MW01286645

How to Make Bath Salts

The Ultimate Guide to Homemade Bath Salts

Table of Contents

Introduction

Bath salts are pulverized water-soluble minerals that are added to your bath water thus its name. Bath salts are said to improve bathing quality and it is said to mimic the natural mineral baths in hot springs and natural baths. As the name implies, bath salts take the appearance of salt crystals but technically speaking, they are far more complex than table salt although it [table salt] is also one of the basic substances used in making bath salt recipes. If you want to make bath salts, then this book is for you. This book will serve as your guide to the wonderful world of bath salts, what you need to know and how to prepare them.

Chapter 1: Bath Salt Basics

Bath salts are simple compounds but they have a lot of benefits to people. This is the reason why many people opt to add bath salts to make them feel relaxed and invigorated. This chapter will teach you what you need to know about bath salts.

Substances Used In Making Bath Salts

There are many types of substances that are labeled as bath salts that you can use. Below are the types of substances that you can use to make bath salts:

Epsom Salt

Epsom salt is an inorganic salt that contains Oxygen, Magnesium and Sulfur It is also called Magnesium sulfate and has a chemical formula of $MgSO_4$. Diluting Magnesium sulfate in water results to a bitter saline taste. It is used in common pharmaceutical preparations as it has many uses such as preventing high blood pressure, decreasing the risk of eclampsia and ease symptoms of asthma to name a few.

Table Salt

Table salt is also called Sodium chloride and it is a good source of iodine. This is especially true among people who suffer from iodine deficiency.

Sodium Hexametaphosphate

Sodium hexametaphosphate is a polymer of Sodium, Oxygen and Phosphorus. It is also called Graham's Salt. It is commonly used as a food additive but it also has beneficial uses. One of the benefits of using Graham salt as bath salt is it provides necessary phosphorus which is a trace element that body's needs in order to function. It is, however, not popularly used in making bath salts.

Dead Sea Salt

Obtained from the Dead Sea, this type of sea salt is considered as the best type of salt for making bath salt recipes. It is rich in rich trace elements and minerals. It is also good in treating inflammations like arthritis, eczema and psoriasis.

Himalayan Pink Salt

Mined from the Himalayan mountains, the Himalayan pink salt is the most expensive and most beneficial of all choices for bath salts. It is good in treating skin rashes like *herpes zoster,* eczema and psoriasis. Moreover, the high concentrations of minerals in bath salts can also help detox the body as well as lower the blood pressure.

History of Bath Salts

The history of bath salts dates as far back as the 2700 B.C. It was first document in China when Peng Tzao Kan Mu released his first publication on using salts to improve the well-being of people after bath. The book described 40 varieties of salts that are no longer used today.

Historical artifacts also indicated that the ancient Egyptians – particularly the rich Egyptians – soaked in mineral-rich waters obtained from the Dead Sea to soften and smoothen their skin. In fact, Egyptians believed that the Dead Sea is a fountain of youth that helps ancient women decrease the appearance of lines and wrinkles in the face.

However, the popularity of bath salts is not only concentrated in China as news of its efficacy have made its way to countries in Europe particularly in Rome and Greece. Famous scholar and healer, Hippocrates, encourages his fellow Greeks to use salt to heal different types of maladies. In fact, the earliest known bath salt is immersing in sea water which Greeks believed to have antimicrobial properties that can heal wounds and other skin ailments.

In Rome, grand baths infused with natural spring water were also constructed to provide relief to different maladies to people. Roman doctor Dioskurided published a book called *De Materia Medica* which discusses the healing properties of salts in treating bites, wounds and digestive problems.

This immense use of bath salts in the ancient world is the reason why English physician and author Charles Russel published a book called *The Uses of Sea Water.* Today, bath salts extend to the present day as many modern spas as well as wellness centers offer salt water treatments and store different types of salt bath treatments for their many clients.

Benefits of Bath Salts

Taking a dip in a tub full of water infused with bath salts is very invigorating. There are many benefits that you can get from bath salts and below are the things that you can get after submerging in bath salts.

- **Helps exfoliate the skin.** There are many bath salts that contain phosphates which have detergent action that can soften the calloused skin. This is true for bath salts that contain baking soda.

- **Helps remove toxins and pollutants in the body.** When submerging yourself in bath salts, the concentration of ions is more in the tub than outside the body thus resulting to osmosis. The high concentration of salts in the tub results to the pulling of water outside the body and, as a result, detoxification occurs.

- **Eases stress.** There is nothing more relaxing than having a dip in bath water infused with bath salts. Aside from easing stress, bath salts can also help improve concentration and sleep.

- **Helps the nerves function properly.** Bath salts is a great treatment for people who suffer from nerve and muscle damage. The minerals that are found in bath salts are very beneficial to the repair of torn muscles and damaged nerves.

- **Reduce the inflammation.** People who suffer from wounds and bruises can take advantage of warm bath salts. Bath salts contain minerals that improve the blood flow within the body thus helping reduce the inflammation fast.

- **Removes dead cells from the skin.** Most bath salts have grainy texture thus the mild abrasive properties of bath salts help remove dead cells from the skin.

Chapter 2: Before Making Bath Salt Recipes

So you are excited to make your own bath salts. However, before you buy the ingredients and prepare the tools, it is important that you equip yourself with the right information to make your bath salt preparation success even if it is your first time.

Main Ingredients in Making Bath Salts

Making bath salt recipes is not only about using the right bath salt. You can make your recipes more interesting if you also use other materials to improve the health benefits that you can get out of bath salts.

Essential Oils

Essential oils are concentrated volatile plant extracts that promote psychological and physical well-being. They often come with very strong yet relaxing aroma that is commonly used in aromatherapy. Essential oils provide the main scent of bath salt recipes.

Dried Herbs

Dried herbs have the same scents as well as healing properties as essential oils. They are great additions to bath salts not only to improve the therapeutic effect but also the texture of the finished product. The drawback of using herbs in bath salts is that they can create a lot of mess if used in the bath tub but if you are using them for foot spa, then the mess is very manageable.

Carrier Oils

Carrier oils are vegetable oils that have moisturizing properties. They are used together with essential oils that are too strong. When using carrier oils, you need to use 12 to 30 drops of essential oil to 1 ounce of carrier oil. Remember that you should only use carrier oil for essential oils that are very strong.

Hydrogen Peroxide

Hydrogen peroxide in water increases the oxygen that is available to the body. Thus if you use it together with the bath salt, you will feel alert as well as revitalized. Aside from providing Oxygen, Hydrogen peroxide also has antibacterial, antifungal and antiviral properties.

Apple Cider Vinegar

Apple cider vinegar is very beneficial to the health as it helps restore the natural pH levels of the skin as well as hair. Moreover, it also helps restore the acid mantle protection of the skin which is usually lost when using soap on the skin. It also has antifungal, antibacterial and antiviral properties.

Citric Acid

Citric acid is a key ingredient for bath bombs which you cans make to make bath salts more interesting. Using citric acid creates effervescence that makes the bath time experience more interesting.

Colorants

Add more interesting color to your bath salts by using colorants such as FD&C dyes or liquid glycerin.

Dendritic Salt

Dendritic salts are ordinary table salts with crystals that have branched into star-like configuration instead of normal cubes. It has high capacity to absorb moisture and it is used to hold the fragrance of bath salts longer.

Corn Starch

Corn starch can also be added to bath salt recipes to give the water a silky feeling.

Sodium Bicarbonate

Sodium bicarbonate is just your ordinary baking soda. Bath salts that contain sodium bicarbonate are especially made for detoxification. Baking soda has alkalizing effect on the body and this is very important among people who suffer from overly acidic blood due to eating too much meat, sugar and refined foods. Baking soda acts as a neutralizer and you will feel refreshed after soaking in your bath infused with this substance.

Sodium Sesquicarbonate

Also called a double salt of Sodium bicarbonate, this substance is commonly used in bath salts and swimming pools. Its high alkaline property makes it good for detoxification. It also helps patients suffering from copper intoxification.

Glycerin

Glycerin is a common ingredient in making bath salts and it is considered as a lubricant, emollient and humefactant when used in other bath salt products.

Tips When Making Bath Salts

Making your own bath salts is very easy and you don't need expensive materials and equipment to start making it so that you can enjoy its benefits afterwards. This section will discuss about the tips on how to make great bath salt recipes.

- **Keep your recipes simple.** The best tip when it comes to making homemade bath salt recipes is to keep the recipes simple. In fact, some of the best homemade bath salts contain natural salt mixed with a little bit of essential oil.

- **Use essential oils and perfumes sparingly.** It is crucial that you use essential oil sparingly when making bath salts. While essential oils are very aromatic, excessive use can often lead to allergic reaction. Remember that essential oils are highly volatile thus too much exposure to it can lead t to burning sensations or allergic reactions.

- **Use textured salt.** The best types of salts to use are textured ones. Table salts and kosher salt are relatively fine grained so they are not good choices for textured salt. Great choices for bath salts include Epsom salts, Dead Sea salt, pink rock salt, grey salt and dendritic salt. However, these types of salts are a bit expensive thus if you are not really that keen about the texture of your salt, then using fine-grained salts is okay.

- **Do not overdo with aromatherapy.** While aromatherapy oil is used in making bath salt recipes, it is important that you do not overdo it. The thing is that aromatherapy oils are designed to dissipate into the air and not soak into the skin so whether you put too little or too much, it does not really give any additional benefits to bath salts.

- **Use the right colorants.** When making bath salts, it is important that you use the right colorants. You may think that food safe dyes are good but it might have extreme consequences such as staining the bathtub or even the bather – that's you. Look for cosmetic-grade pigments and dye to add to your bath salt.

- **Store the bath salt in airtight containers.** To prevent the fragrance of your bath salt recipes from dissipating, make sure that you store them inside airtight containers. Moreover, it will also help if you store the containers away from direct sunlight. Exposure to sunlight and heat may change the chemical composition of the bath salt.

Making bath salts is a great thing that you can do to improve your bath time experience. Make sure that you follow these tips so that you will become successful in making your very own bath salt recipes.

Chapter 3: Bath Salt Recipes

Bath salt recipes are very easy to make. The best thing about making homemade bath salts is that you can customize your very own recipe depending on your preferences. There are many bath salt recipes that you can try and this chapter will share with you great bath salt recipes to treat different conditions.

Basic Bath Salt Recipe

This is an essential bath salt recipe that you need to know. It is a very simple recipe that you can use and the best thing is that the ingredients are found inside your kitchen.

Ingredients:
Dried leaves or flowers
½ cup baking soda
30 to 60 drops of essential oil of your choice
3 cups of Epsom salt (can be substituted with Epsom salt)

Directions:

1.) In a mixing bowl, mix all ingredients.
2.) Use a wooden spoon to incorporate all ingredients.
3.) Put the mixture inside a container with an airtight lid.
4.) Store in a cool, dark and dry place.
5.) To use, get half a cup of the mixture and place in the bath water.

Bath Salt Glow

This bath salt recipe contains essential oil and Vitamin E that helps rejuvenate the skin's youthful glow. It is a great bath salt recipe that can help you bring back supple skin.

Ingredients:
20 to 30 drops of essential oil blend
1 tablespoon D-alpha Tocopherol (Vitamin E)
2 oz Avocado oil
4 oz Grapeseed oil
½ cup Fine-grained sea salt
½ cup Dead Sea salt (fine-grained)

Directions:

1.) In a mixing bowl, mix the two salts together. Mix well using a spoon.
2.) Add the ingredients together and make sure to incorporate the mixture well.
3.) Pour the mixture in a glass jar with airtight seal.
4.) To use, pour ¼ cup of the bath salt into a tub full of warm water.
5.) Mix well before soaking in the tub.

Bath Tea

This interesting bath salt recipe is contained inside tea bags thus making the application more novel and mess-free. This is something that you should try to make to make your bath time more fun and less messy. You can substitute the tea bags with organza or muslin bags if you cannot find any.

Ingredients:
3" x 5" tea bags
Dried chamomile flowers
Dried lavender flowers
12 drops of Orange essential oil
½ cup Grey salt

Directions:

1.) In a mixing bowl, pour the Grey salt and add the essential oil. Mix the two ingredients together.
2.) Add the dried flowers and herbs and continue to mix until incorporated well.
3.) Fill the tea bag with at least 4 ounces of the mixture.
4.) Pack the tea bags individually inside small Ziploc plastic bags to preserve the scent and avoid the salts from drying out too much.
5.) To use, toss one tea bag into a warm bath water. Wait for a few minutes until the tea bag seeps into the water and the salt melts.

6.) The best thing about this recipe is that you can re-use the tea bags for your next bath.

Salt Scrub

This is a great salt scrub that you can try. You can use it for foot spa or as a massage bath salt to exfoliate your skin. The Dead Sea salt also contains high amounts of minerals that the body can benefit from. It is a simple recipe that anyone can do.

Ingredients:
5 to 15 drops of any essential oil blend
½ cup Jojoba oil or any type of massage oil
1 cup Dead Sea salt

Directions:

1.) In a mixing bowl, combine all ingredients and mix well using a spoon or a spatula.
2.) To use, simply rub an ample amount of the bath salt scrub to the skin before showering.

Crystal Bath Salt Potpourri

Make this crystal bath salt potpourri for your bath time. It can function as bath salts as well as cute décor in your bathroom.

Ingredients:
Essential oil or any fragrance oil of your choice
A drop of liquid-based colorant (Mica powder)
Sea Salt crystals

Directions:

1.) In a mixing bowl, add all the ingredients and blend well using a wooden spoon or spatula.
2.) Wear hand gloves and scoop out a ball of the salt mixture and place on the parchment paper to dry.
3.) Let it air dry for several hours of days if needed.
4.) To use, just drop a few crystals into the bath water and wait for the bath salts to dissolve.

Bath Bomb

Bath bombs are interesting bath salt recipes that can make your bath time more fun. It releases effervescence during bath time.

Ingredients:
Dried herbs (optional)
Essential oil blend
Witch hazel
2 ½ cups baking soda
1 ¼ cups Citric Acid
1 cup Sea salt (fine-grained)

Directions:

1.) In a mixing bowl, combine all of the dry ingredients.
2.) Use a wooden spoon to incorporate everything.
3.) Prepare the bath salt molds. You can use a muffin pan or an ice cube tray that you don't use anymore.
4.) Place the dried herbs at the bottom of the mold.
5.) Put a tiny amount of witch hazel or essential oil to soften the dry mixture.
6.) As soon as the mixture can hold its shape, place them inside the mold.
7.) Let the bath salts dry in the mold for a few hours.

8.) Put in airtight plastic bags.

9.) To use, drop one bath bomb in the bath water and enjoy the magic unravel in front of your eyes.

Oatmeal Bath Salt

This oatmeal bath salt recipe is wonderfully refreshing for the skin. The addition of oatmeal adds texture to the bath salt that gives bathers a great experience.

Ingredients:
½ oz lavender essential oil
1 ½ cups pulverized oatmeal
1 cup sea salt
2 cups Epsom salt

Directions:

1.) In a bowl, mix all the ingredients together and break up large clumps.
2.) Make sure that the oatmeal is well incorporated in the bath salt.
3.) Store inside an airtight jar.
4.) To use, get a scoop of the bath salt and rub it on your skin before showering.
5.) Rinse thoroughly.

Bath Salts for Stuffy Nose

This bath salt is aromatic and it also serves as a therapeutic recipe for people who are lethargic and are suffering from stuffy nose.

Ingredients:
10 drops of peppermint essential oil
2 drops of pine cedar oil
2 drops of tea tree essential oil
3 drops of lavender essential oil
4 drops of eucalyptus essential oil
2 cups baking soda
2 cups sea salt
2 cups Epsom salt

Directions:

1.) In a mixing bowl, add all ingredients together except the essential oils and break up any clumps using a wooden spoon.
2.) Add the essential oils last and mix everything in.
3.) Scoop the bath salt into jars with airtight lids.
4.) To use, add a spoonful of bath salt in a tub full of warm water and soak for a few minutes. Be sure to inhale the aroma to ease your stuffy nose.

Foot Soak Bath Salt Recipe

Bath salts are also great for foot soak or foot spa. This recipe is also a great way to treat people suffering from athlete's foot and inflamed joints.

Ingredients:
40 drops of peppermint essential oil
4 drops of tea tree essential oil
4 drops of lavender essential oil
1 cup baking soda
2 cups sea salt
2 cups Epsom salt

Directions:

1.) Mix the dry ingredients in a mixing bowl. Use a wooden spoon to incorporate all ingredients.
2.) Add the essential oils last and incorporate all ingredients well.
3.) Put the finished product inside sealed jars and store in a cool and dry place.
4.) Use half a cup of the bath salt recipe in a basin of hot water.
5.) Soak your feet and dry them well after.

Bath Salt for Back Pain Relief

If you are suffering from tired and achy muscles on your back, then you can make your own bath salt recipe to treat you back pain. This bath salt recipe is one of the many things that you can do to relieve yourself from pain. It is a cheaper alternative that you should try today.

Ingredients:
3 tablespoon chamomile flowers, dried
¼ teaspoon chamomile essential oil
½ teaspoon lavender essential oil
3 tablespoon Dendritic salt
1 cup Dead Sea salt
1 cup Epsom salt

Directions:

1.) Put the Dead Sea salt and Epsom salt in a glass mixing bowl. Mix together and set aside.
2.) In another glass bowl, put the Dendritic salt and add the chamomile and lavender essential oils. Blend well until the oils are incorporated to the salt.
3.) Mix all of the ingredients including the dried chamomile flowers.
4.) To use, get half a cup of the bath salt and place it in a tub full of warm water. Soak in the bath everyday to get the desired result.

Lemon Bath Salt

This bath salt recipe is very aromatic and it also provides relaxation to people who are stressed out or are feeling anxiety and depression.

Ingredients:
½ teaspoon vanilla extract
½ teaspoon lemon essential oil
3 tablespoon Dendritic salt
1 cup Epsom salt
1 cup fine-grained seas salt

Directions:

1.) In a glass mixing bowl, mix together the sea salt and Epsom salt then set aside.
2.) In another bowl, mix together the Dendritic salt and the lemon essential oil and vanilla extract.
3.) Combine all ingredients and place inside a glass bottle with airtight lid.
4.) To use, get half a cup of the bath salt and place in a tub filled with warm water. Soak in the tub until you feel relaxed.

Invigorating Epsom Bath Salt

This quick and easy bath salt recipe is very convenient to make and also easier to customize. The Epsom salt which serves as the base ingredient of this bath salt soothes the nerves.

Ingredients:
2 tablespoon olive oil
1 drop peppermint essential oil
2 drops sage essential oil
1 cup Epsom salt

Directions:

1.) Combine all ingredients in a glass mixing bowl.
2.) Use a wooden spoon to mix all ingredients together.
3.) Put the finished product inside a clean jar with airtight lid.
4.) To use the bath salt, use half a cup and pour it in a tub full of warm water.

Sparkling Bath Salt

This sparkling bath salt recipes does not only look attractive but it is also jam-packed with healing properties that can help alleviate pain from sore muscles.

Ingredients:
¼ cup ground mint
1 cup rock salt
2 tablespoon preferred essential oil
1 cup Epsom salt
1 cup cornstarch

Directions:

1.) In a glass bowl, add all the ingredients together but make sure to add the cornstarch last.
2.) Place the mixture in a glass jar with a tight-fitting lid and store inside a cool and dry place.
3.) Scoop half a cup of the bath salt mixture and place it in warm water. Notice that the cornstarch will start to thicken the water which provides a more silky feel to the bather.

Eucalyptus Spearmint Bath Salt

This bath salt recipe is infused with the relaxing aroma of eucalyptus and spearmint.

Ingredients:
3 drops eucalyptus essential oil
3 drops spearmint essential oil
¼ cup baking soda
1 cup Epsom salt

Directions:

1.) Combine the baking soda and Epsom salt in a small bowl and mix until well blended.
2.) Add the essential oils and mix well.
3.) Place the essential oils in a mixing bowl.
4.) You can also add green coloring to the bath salt to make it more attractive.
5.) To use, pour half a cup of the bath salt to a tub full of warm water. Soak for at least thirty minutes to get the desired effect.

Silky Bath Salt Scrub

This bath salt recipe serves a dual function for aromatherapy and exfoliation. It is a bath salt recipe that you can easily prepare right at the comforts of your home.

Ingredients:
¼ cup Epsom salt
1 cup sea salt
1 teaspoon vanilla extract
2 tablespoon rose oil
¼ cup baby oil (optional)
¼ cup coconut oil
½ cup extra virgin coconut oil

Directions:

1.) In a saucepan, pour the coconut oil, extra virgin olive oil, baby oil, vanilla extract and rose oil. Heat over medium heat until the oil begins to boil. Keep stirring and remove from the heat. Set aside.
2.) In a mixing bowl, mix together Epsom salt and sea salt. Mix well. Pour the cooled oil into the salt and continue mixing until well combined. If the salt falls at the bottom and the oil rises, then you are doing the right thing.
3.) You can add uncooked oatmeal and reduce salt if the bath salt is too strong.

4.) Place inside an airtight container and store inside a dry and dark place.

Rose Oat Milk Bath Salt

This wonderfully aromatic bath salt provides relaxations and renewed energy to anyone who uses it.

Ingredients:
A handful of ground rose petals
15 drops of rose essential oil
1 cup milk powder
1 cup oat powder
1 cup sea salt
2 cups Epsom salt

Directions:

1.) Mix all the dry ingredients in a glass mixing bowl. Use a spoon to mix all the ingredients in.
2.) Add the scent and mix again to incorporate the scent to the rest of the ingredients.
3.) Add the rose petals and mix.
4.) Place the mixture inside a glass jar with tight lid.

Orange Lemongrass Bath Salt

This orange and lemongrass bath salt is great for relaxation. Moreover, the Epsom salt that it contains also help fight off inflammation, bruising and wounds.

Ingredients:
A handful of calendula flowers
6 drops lemongrass essential oil
8 drops orange essential oil
1 cup milk powder
1 cup oat powder
1 cup sea salt
2 cups Epsom salt

Directions:

1.) Mix all the dry ingredients first in a bowl.
2.) Sift to remove the clumps.
3.) Add the scent and incorporate the mixture well using a spoon.
4.) Add the calendula flowers last and mix again.
5.) Store the mixture inside a glass jar with airtight lid.

Lilac, Gardenia and Almond Bath Salt

This bath salt recipe is infused with the sweet smelling aroma of lilac, gardenia and almond. You would want to soak in this bath for a long time.

Ingredients:
5 tablespoon almond oil
8 drops gardenia oil
8 drops lilac essential oil
1 cup milk powder
1 cup oat powder
1 cup Himalayan pink salt (sea salt may be substituted)
2 cups Epsom salt

Directions:

1.) Mix all the dry ingredients well.
2.) Sift to remove any clumps then add the essential oil.
3.) Mix again until well incorporated.
4.) Store inside a glass jar and cover.
5.) To use, get half a cup of the bath salt mixture and put in a bath tub filled with warm water.

Chamomile Lavender and Calendula Bath Salts

This bath salt recipe is sure to make you feel relaxed as soon as you immerse yourself in bath water. It can also be used as a foot soak to ease tired feet.

Ingredients:
8 to 10 drops of lavender essential oil
A handful of calendula flowers
½ cup ground chamomile flowers
1 cup milk powder
1 cup oat powder
1 cup sea salt
2 cups Epsom salt

Directions:

1.) Put all the dry ingredients in a mixing bowl.
2.) Blend well until the ingredients are incorporated.
3.) Add the scent.
4.) Mix in the flowers and store the mixture inside a glass jar with air tight lid.

Milky Oatmeal Bath Salt

Bath salts can also be customized to make this interesting recipe. This milky oatmeal bath salt comes with an interesting texture that you should not miss.

Ingredients:
½ cup milk
2 drops of essential oil
½ cup regular oatmeal
2 cups Epsom salt

Directions:

1.) Place all ingredients (except the essential oil) inside a blender to pulverize.
2.) Set the blender to pulse until you achieve the consistency of a fine beach sand.
3.) Add the essential oil last.
4.) Place the mixture inside a container with an air-tight lid.
5.) Store in a dry and dark place.
6.) To use, get a few spoonfuls of the mixture and mix in the bath water.

There are many other bath salt recipes that you can try. There are thousands of bath salt recipes that you can try. However, you can make your very own recipe to meet your preferences. The best thing about making bath salts is that you can use your creativity to create something that will make you truly enjoy your bath time experience.

Conclusion

Immersing yourself in a tub full of water infused with bath salts can be very relaxing. Making your own bath salt is very easy and all there is to it is to get the right ingredients and also be creative. Fortunately, the ingredients used in making bath salts are found in your kitchen so you can whip up a new batch of bath salts out of whim. With these bath salt recipes, your bath time will never be boring and you might find yourself in your tub more often than you are used to. So go on and make your bath salt recipes today!

Made in the USA
Lexington, KY
09 December 2016